A personal journey in to
Earning Trust and Leading others

Table of Contents.

I0493545

Preface

When I was 17 years old, we were having dinner at home, as usual, my three brothers, my parents and I. My eldest brother had graduated University as an Accountant and was working at Thomson McLintock as an Auditor. He started to have a conversation about taxation with my father, dull for sure, but nevertheless a man to man conversation. The looks on both their faces spelled out that the relationship had changed. They were more like equals and the attention that my father paid to Mike sold me. At that moment I could describe to you what I wanted – the same. Sadly a few years later, before I could get my 'career' going, my father sadly passed. I never got to have that conversation and to this day, it's all I have ever wanted. This book is the culmination of years of learning that, when finished; I hope would have made my Dad proud.

Andrew

It won't come as a surprise that when asked, participants on a leadership program, name trust as the number one requirement of a great leader, or a leader they perceive from history who was great, Usually Mandela, Obama, Churchill, Hitler, Ghandi and so on. It will also probably not come as a surprise to find that trust indices, across much of the world, are in serious decline. In fact, over the last ten years, and probably more, we have learned not to trust our politicians, more recently we have learned not to trust our bankers and increasingly we are being given reasons not to trust our business leaders. In many cases, even the organisations that we commit ourselves to during employment, can show reasons why we should not trust our senior leaders. If trust is the first word that often is spoken by employees when asked what they want from their leaders and yet, the results show that they are not feeling that they can trust their leaders, it becomes abundantly clear that there is a gap.

What follows are the principles of the 4C's approach to Leadership. Not a model but a Toolbox. One that can be used very day to build trust with employees, customers, anyone. They can even be used in the home. These tools are there to be chosen for their applicability to differing situations and familiarity with them, their uses and how to apply them will give you the strongest communication tools you could want to find.

I don't set myself out as an icon of Leadership. I just think from what I've learned over the course of career is worth sharing. I say career very loosely, I haven't had so much of a career, rather than a succession of interesting jobs.

I started out at college learning to cook (something which I still do and enjoy, I think I'm pretty good too) and learning the hospitality trade. I left home and worked in a couple of hotels doing everything, cooking, cleaning, waiting on, and even some management duties. By the third hotel I was cooking at people's tables (a chance to 'show off') and running the restaurant coupled with night porter duties and anything else that needed doing. In hindsight, it wasn't the owner who asked or even inspired me to do so much, I think it was out of respect for the team, it had to be done so we shared everything. Plus – it was fun!

I then moved in to the world of pubs and for 3 years ran a very successful pub/restaurant in a forgotten resort town and with my team of 60, we turned over £1million in our first full year. I'm pretty sure I never led the team in the real sense, but allowed them to do what they did best. I had to manage staff from time to time, but largely all the credit goes down to the team.

Later in my 'career' whilst working at Warner Bros I got my first real taste of leadership. Leading the charge on a cultural reform that went right across the business, but I still had a lot to learn.

Ten years ago I was lucky enough to be working alongside some of the world's leading Leadership commentators including Terry Pearce, from the HASS Business School, UCLA at Berkeley and author of 'Leading out Loud'. From Terry, I learned a lot and with my prior experiences from the past to lean on and his teachings and guidance, I finally formed my own Leadership advocacy.

The same will apply to you, we are all different, seven and half billion of us! Your approach will differ to mine and you will use the tools differently, and some you will be more comfortable with than others. What I'd ask you to do is try one or two of them on for size and if they don't fit, try them again later. Practice is the art of perfecting and if you don't try and persist, they won't work for you.

Andrew

Chapter Two - Trust

"Trust is a fragile thing - difficult to build, easy to break. It cannot be bargained for. Only if it is freely given it can be expected in return"

Peter Lerangis

So why is trust in Leadership so important? Surely we can just tell people to do what we need them to and 'performance manage' them if they don't do it right. We have all seen plenty of cases of success from business leaders who have adopted this approach with great gusto and go on to continually achieve outstanding success. Alan Sugar, Donald Trump, even Steve Jobs has been noted as somewhat of an autocrat. What's wrong with adopting that style? The American journalist David Harsanyi is quoted as saying, "Aside from the occasional genocide, oppression, evil and torture, etc., it is inarguable that public policy could be implemented more rapidly in an autocracy" and you know he may well be right. We could also argue that an autocracy damages the sustainability of a venture; yet, Trump, Amstrad and Apple seem to be doing okay. The Caudwell group under John Caudwell did just fine, leaving him to retire with an ample pot. Trust has a place in an autocracy as well as a democracy, partially since Trust can be founded on consistency, consistency of who you are and how you behave. Sadly, most of us are aware of at least one manager with whom we have worked that demonstrates at least one inconsistency between their 'talk' and their 'walk'. When such an inconsistency exists between actions and words, no one is able to anticipate behaviour, which often drives individuals' from interactions when not entirely necessary due to fear of reactions. This separation due to a lack of trust can result in inefficiency, and unfulfilled potential, something that should be avoided, particularly in the work place.

Of course, one reason why Trust is so important is our rapidly changing business landscape with generation Y employees (those aged between 18 and 30) fast becoming the majority of all potential employees, despite an ageing population, makes the need for change is even more pronounced. Time magazine described them as the 'Me, Me, Me' generation. They do not want to be told what to do, they want to be a part of it, in fact, they are probably less interested in running <u>your</u> business, and far more likely to be interested in running a business of their own at some point. They want leadership in the workplace and they want to trust in leaders, but they want it styled in their way. Therefore, it follows that the autocratic styles of leadership of our youth are no longer relevant in today's employer market and as leaders, we have to find new ways of engaging employees in our projects or businesses, ways that serve to seek the new ideology of our fast emerging workforce and above all, to demonstrate trustworthiness.

So what do we mean by Trust? The first thing to note is that, how each person trusts depends upon his or her own particular lens. Some trust openly, until someone or something betrays that trust. Others tend to be more sceptical before trusting others, preferring to wait for the evidence that someone or something is trustworthy. So much depends, according to the psychologists, upon what we experienced in our formative years.

Trust is contextual. Some individuals we trust because we know them or they have proven themselves over time to be consistent in behaviour. These individuals we tend to trust since we believe we can anticipate their behaviour. Other individuals we 'warm to them' or like their personality, but without getting to know these individuals we are highly unlikely to display a high degree of trust; such as trusting them with our child.

That said, we've already talked about consistency of behaviour and add to that a consistency between who we are and the person we show up to work as. Historically we have been encouraged to leave our emotions at home and not bring them to work. Does that encourage inconsistencies between who we really are and how we show up?

To find out more and about other characteristics that make up Trustworthiness, we need to look at leaders we do or have trusted OR those we haven't or do not. While previously we have mentioned inconsistency in talk and walk (action) as a problem in trust development, we must add to that the need for consistency between who we really are, and the person that we appear to be when at work. Falling into the category of being 'real', true to oneself, or authentic, when colleagues or subordinates notice any degree of inconsistency between your behaviour in the office and your personal behaviour, any trust that you have built up will be tarnish since they may not 'understand who you are anymore.'

In a recent Edelman Trust Barometer results for trust in Governments, they recorded a nine point drop in the worldwide total, giving an overall score of only 43% of the population trusting in their Governments. In the UK, trust fell from 43% in 2011 to 38% in 2012, potentially due to David Cameron? In the US, there was a 7 point uplift in trust to 49%, potentially due to Barack Obama? Maybe, but there are too many variables to be sure if there is a connection to national political leadership. Nevertheless, in a recent Readers Digest survey of the top American notable people concerning whom they trust Barack Obama came in 65th, just behind Adam Sandler, the actor and comedian. Tom Hanks came in first.

After researching the psychologists' view of Trust, so much has to do with a sense of 'connection'. Having a moment of truth with another individual, we naturally get either a positive or negative feeling – an emotion if you will. Some may feel that the particular moment affirms that trust exists, whilst in another situation the moment may fuel the scepticism or doubt that we feel. Trusting somebody from a distance, like Barack Obama, is difficult because we have so few (if any) opportunities to make any emotional connections and resort to replace these connections with the moments we read about somebody, or see them make a speech. It's the same with Tom Hanks. We've seen him on TV as himself and we've made emotional connections with his characters, and so we feel like we know him enough to trust him.

The same can be true of our business leaders, bankers and politicians. As media has become faster, more intrusive, we have greater opportunities to make these virtual connections with people. We watch corporate videos of our CEO's, see them in the press. We are starting to make judgements about who they are and how consistent they are being. Trouble is, for the most part, leaders leave it all to guess work. For some leaders, the increased openness about themselves in their professional as well as private lives boosts how others view them, while for some leaders this openness has revealed more inconsistencies creating further scepticism from individuals.

Sharing more about ourselves, who we really are, creates more intimate relationships between leaders and followers, assuming that the leader is present or at least visible. This intimacy can remove the guesswork, allowing employees to know their leaders beyond their job titles, giving employees an opportunity to gauge for themselves the extent to which they feel that their leaders are being consistent. Seeing leaders as being consistent in their words, actions and deeds with who they are, we could call authenticity.

There has been much written over recent years about Authentic Leadership, and with good reason. The leading commentators such as Terry Pearce, Bill George, and Rob Goffee & Gareth Jones have put the subject of authenticity firmly on the leadership map. Furthermore, the writings of Daniel Goldman about EQ (Emotional Quotient) have further developed the field of leadership capability and EQ is now considered THE leading predictor of future Leadership capability.

In December 2011, Sunderland Football club were languishing in the relegation zone of the premiership football table, yet in that month they replaced their Manager. Under Martin O'Neill, Sunderland began to improve dramatically with four wins from his first six games, including one over league leaders' Manchester City. Sunderland continued to perform well in the first few months under O'Neill. They rose to ninth in the league and continued their challenge for a Europa League spot. On 18 February, they beat Arsenal 2–0 to knock them out of the FA Cup fifth round. Sunderland's form petered out at the end of the season and after no wins in the last 8 games but they finished a respectable 13th place, a position Sunderland fans would've been happy with after the start to the season. What brought about such an immediate change in fortunes?

The point here being that the players clearly had the ability to win, but it was not until a change in leadership that it was evident in their performance. It was almost as if the team were holding back their true potential until inspired to do so.

Over the last two decades, there has been lots of research concerning Leadership and the requirements placed upon leaders, formally or informally, by employees. Of course what shows up when you identify what Senior Leaders are good at; they are good at their job, are competent, good at decision making and taking responsibility for their actions. The skills of senior leaders are all the things that you'd expect, which affirms all the reasons why they got the job with the corner office in the first place! Yet. Ask employees what they want from a leader; you'll get trustworthiness, empathy and meaning. Sure they still want their leaders to be good at their job, but these more inspiring characteristics of Trust. Empathy and Meaning, 'making human connections' take precedence. Employees want to trust their leaders; they want to know that their leaders' care about them, especially in these times since the financial crisis has brought about so much uncertainty. And they want to know why their job matters – they want more meaning in their work. Considering the previous expansion on generation Y in the workplace, leaders need to encapsulate more than just ability to do their job, but the ability to assuage subordinates into producing to the best of their abilities, through appealing to employees at a personal level.

Keep thinking of your trustworthiness as a bank account, the more tools you use, you top up your trust bank balance, and every time you don't do something to reinforce your trustworthiness, your balance goes down.

The big challenge with trust is that it's an emotion. It's very hard to mandate an emotion. Typically, we manifest our beliefs, valuea and emotions in behaviours, so therefore we can only influence emotions by changing our behaviours and subsequently trying to influence the emotions of others. Tricky!

Finally, trust others. As Andrew Fowler, Human Resources Director at Kantar Worldpanel will tell you, "I trust everyone in my team and they pay me back with their trust in me." One of Andrew's team, Ian Negus says "Andrew just trusts us and that is why we follow him". You recruit people to do the things you can't or don't have time for. You hopefully recruit people who can do things better than you can. So no more "if you want something done properly, do it yourself" – if you want something done well, get someone who can do a great job, let them get on it with it – trust them. You'll be rewarded for relinquishing control and trusting others.

Chapter 3 – Leadership

Before we can move in to the world of creating trust as a leader, we need to establish what we mean by leadership. There are literally hundreds of quotes, a mountain of research and theories, all of which very credible and relevant. I'd like to be very simple for the purposes of clarity.

When you choose to lead, and it is a choice, you are seeking the committed support from your team or constituents, to take the actions that you need them to in order to achieve your goal or goals.

Leadership is but one of a range of tools that you can deploy to get things done. For example:

Delegation – "here's what I need doing, go and do it."

Direction – "the building is on fire, get out!"

Motivating – Providing some form of incentive or dis-incentive for actions.

Leadership – Inspiring others to want to carry out required actions.

So when you choose to use Leadership as your tool to get things done, you need to inspire your potential followers to action. The word inspire comes from the Latin word *inspirare* meaning to breathe. More latterly we mean to animate someone with an emotion. So to breathe an emotion in to someone is what you're seeking to do.

"At the end of the day people won't remember what you said or did, they will remember how you made them feel."

Maya Angelou

This provides us with both a challenge and an opportunity. If we can tap in to the emotions of ourselves (the opportunity) and breathe that emotion in to others (the challenge) we hope for the expected outcome that our teams and constituents will do what we need them to, not because we told them to, but because they want to.

What do we mean by emotions? Well in the context of the world of work we're probably taking about a finite list emotions. We may want people to feel excited about a project or task; to feel the sense of urgency; passionate about the customer; fearful of possible outcomes; frustration with how things are now; optimistic about the future.   What would it be like if your team or entire workforce were excited about coming to work?

I know I have had several jobs where I was less than excited to go to work, we all have. What happens is we don't give enough of ourselves, we do what is required. The difference between enough work and great work is how much we are willing to contribute of ourselves – our discretionary effort.   The job of the leader is to move people beyond what it says in the job description and tap in to peoples' discretionary effort – to do great work; to act as an ambassador for the company; to exceed customer expectations; to work as a team; and ultimately contribute to organisational success and intent.

Identifying how a situation make us feel is the first step to inspiring others. You NEED to look inside yourself and understand how you feel – if you don't know how you feel about a given situation, you can't breathe that feeling in to others OR if you can't get yourself inspired, you have no hope of inspiring others.

We have to tap in to our own emotions, what makes us excited about coming to worker challenge. Emotions like excitement are contagious and if we can spread that about – Wow!

When I ran the pub/restaurant, the first thing done was a complete refurbishment and as I watched the pans unfold, I was really excited about the potential of the site – the colours and the dreams I had. I shared them every day with the staff as we converted this drab old building inn to something vibrant and entertaining. I think, you'll have to ask them, it was this excitement that fired the staff up to make the most of what we had been given.

I developed the 4C toolbox to help you do just that. It's a set of questions to help you tap in to what emotions you're feeling. It's a tool box to help others connect with the problem and buy in to the solution. It's also a toolbox that helps you communicate with others in a way that, given sufficient information, they can choose to what extent they are willing to subscribe to your actions.

Finally, it is a toolbox that can be used to boost your trust bank account and be the trusted leader.

The 4C's are simply:

Context – What is happening right now that needs to change and what will it look like once we make the changes.

Credibility – I want to follow the smartest person who can deliver what needs to be delivered. Why should you be the one to follow?

Character - Who are you? What is about you that makes you special and worthy of my commitment?

Communication – Leadership can be a lonely place and frankly communication is the only tool in your toolbox. Use it well and reap the rewards.

Chapter 4: Context

You can't connect the dots looking forward; you can only connect them looking backwards. So you have to trust that the dots will somehow connect in your future. You have to trust in something - your gut, destiny, life, karma, whatever. This approach has never let me down, and it has made all the difference in my life.

Steve Jobs

People are naturally emotional and often quite passionate about the work that they do. Ask anyone what they do for a living and demonstrate a high level of curiosity, and watch them become animated about what they do, unless of course they hate their job! This is logical due to the amount of time that an individual invests in their work, whether it is a position utilising their maximum potential or a job that only utilises a portion of present potential. We have also seen that people want to be able to contribute to the greater whole. They want to find their work meaningful and worthwhile. The creation of a compelling definition of success is paramount to be able to excite peoples' desires to contribute. You can imagine, for example, when Graeme Lowdon and John Booth quit Manor Formula 1 racing and moved in to the world of Endurance Racing 1 imagine that they did not have any trouble forming a team of willing engineers to contribute to their project. Or even NASA, when JFK stated that, "This nation should dedicate itself to achieving the goal, before this decade is out, of landing a man on the moon and returning him safely to Earth." I bet they would have had a busy time in the recruiters' office for NASA during the next 9 years for such an inspiring project.

Projects of huge technical interest or of great noble intent are readily primed to create a sense of a compelling future, but what about the project team working to implement a new payroll system or to win a large client bid or remove layers from a top-heavy organisation? That's not to under-estimate the significance of those projects to the host organisation, but to make them so compelling requires thought, preparation and careful communication to ensure that the right people are engaged, or 'turned on' by such a task.

The first step to creating such a compelling future is to ensure absolute clarity about what it is you intend to achieve and that means possibly going beyond the mundane of shareholder value or increased EBITDA, it means tapping in to the senses to see what will be different. What will you hear, see, smell, taste as a result of the success from achieving the goal that you share? Being able to define and describe the moment of triumph is of paramount importance and it should somehow, be exciting.

It's a well-established NLP (Neuro Linguistic Programming) tool, often cited by sportsmen and women that use the technique to visualize their moment of triumph. Jack Nicklaus is quoted saying

"I never hit a shot, not even in practice, without having a very sharp, in-focus picture of it in my head. First I see the ball where I want it to finish, nice and white and sitting up high on the bright green grass. Then the scene quickly changes, and I see the ball going there; its path, trajectory, and shape, even its behaviour on landing. Then there is a sort of fade-out, and the next scene shows me making the kind of swing that will turn the previous images into reality."

The same is true in business. If you want others to see or feel the temptation of the moment of celebration it will be up to you to help create that imagery for them. After all, we know that a shared goal is great for teamwork, a shared goal that is consistent in all its team-members will be even more powerful. In the 1960's when Bill Bowerman and Phil Knight pledged that they would "Crush Adidas", they nearly did, as Adidas disappeared from our sports store shelves in the late 1970's and it took some time to come back. Nike, to this day, are just about the pre-eminent sportswear brand on the planet.

Creating that kind of picture can take on many forms such as:
A target – Become a $125 billion company by the year 2000 (Wal-Mart, 1990)
In taking on a Common enemy - Crush Adidas (Nike, 1960s)
To align to a role model - Become the Nike of the cycling industry (Giro Sport Design, 1986)

Or an internal transformation - Transform this company from a defence contractor into the best diversified high-technology company in the world. (Rockwell, 1995)

And it doesn't stop there. Leaders need to constantly remind people why they are there, giving a greater sense of meaning to the teams' efforts. In 1995, when Stewart Miller took over the helm of Whitbread Pub Partnerships, a leased pub operator, he declared that he wanted to achieve "100 percent lessee endorsement of the partnership". This was a clear intention that the value added to individual men and women, that ran their own businesses, from Whitbread, the brewing giant, was to be the competitive advantage over other leased pub operators. His special skill was to tie everything that an employee did to that vision and reminded everyone in his team, several times a day if necessary, what that vision was. Stewart was a tough leader but ahead of so many others when it came to providing a reason how employees' work added value to the overall vision.

Another important aspect of aligning and exciting people to your goals is ensuring that you have absolute clarity about what you want to achieve and being able to communicate that, often, as Stewart did, being able to translate that to anyone within the organization. This requires practice and brevity. Brevity without losing clarity and meaning is difficult to achieve instantly. Blaise Pascal wrote "I have only made this letter longer because I have not had the time to make it shorter." And Mark Twain "If I'd had more time I'd have written shorter letters". It's the elevator pitch!

Jack Welch's, GE's CEO, vision of "being first or second in the markets that they served" led to huge scale restructure, shedding those businesses where that goal was unachievable and great investment to the other businesses. Simple, brief, and yet, powerful.

We've all heard the story of Joe Saltzer, a cleaner at NASA who, when asked what he was doing, declared, "I'm helping put a man on the moon." Possibly urban myth and yet such a powerful story goes a long long way to describe the potential for translating such a simple, concise message, to everyone within a team, no matter how big or how disparate.

Of course, having a message and communicating it is great. To make it really compelling is say why. What underpins this new direction, this change, this strategy? Ideally, whatever sits behind the changes you're advocating can act as the glue that binds everyone together to achieve this goal that you have set.

Simon Sinek wasn't wrong when he wrote 'start with why'. When Anita Roddick started the Bodyshop in 1976, she chose 'to dedicate our business to the pursuit of social and environmental change' and the 'green' philosophies became the hallmark of the quickly growing company, largely indebted to her mother who recycled everything, more due to necessity in the post-war years.

Why, is the second, or probably the first step in providing a context for followers. It can simple be the benefits of taking action, and sometimes even more powerful, can be the consequences of not taking action.

"Why this, why now" goes a long way to helping others see their work and meaningful, and not just the pursuit of a goal, but something with real purpose behind it. Leadership is a contact sport and that requires you to be 'in touch' with your people AND for them to be in touch with your purpose and that means helping others see and feel the current context so that they can align themselves more effectively to the goals and become advocates themselves.

Head back a few years to when you were doing your high school or secondary exams. In Mathematics, you gained extra credits for showing how you worked out your answer, even if the answer itself was incorrect. Helping others see and feel how you got to the answers that you have by showing them how you worked it out.

To those you're communicating to, you'll need to anticipate and acknowledge what they're thinking, their concerns, doubts, feeling and thoughts. What are the implications of the changes that you're advocating on those to whom you are communicating? If it concerns Job security, increased workload, pay freeze, then it is time for a little honesty. If you are not honest there'll be elephants in the room. In business it is best to get such elephants out on the table. They might not thank you for it, but it'll hush the tell-tale whispers of dissent. You'll need to be able to share your thoughts, demonstrate how you came to your conclusions and answer as many questions as people have. As with any maths exam, show them how you got your answers will always gain you partial credit, show them that you looked and investigated alternatives. Show them that you considered all possibilities before ending with your conclusion.

People are likely going to want to know, not just the checks and balances of why you're advocating a change, But to truly connect and inspire people to carry out the tasks that you ask of them, be prepared to give a little more of yourself. For example if you are communicating substantial changes, people naturally are likely going to want to know more than just the checks and balances. In order to truly connect and inspire people to carry out the tasks that you are going to ask of them, you must be prepared to give a little more of yourself and avoid falling in to the trap that others may perceive that there is self-interest at work here.
It's tricky, I know at Warner Bros I had taken my family out to the movie theatre and as most people do, you go to the nearest as

long as you can get you want, parking, maybe some restaurants nearby. I told them that I would be so proud to see a time when people would drive past other theatres to go to a Warner Theatre just because of the experience they would get and why? Because I'd know I had succeeded.

Try asking yourself the question: why do you care about the changes that you're advocating? If your answer is in anyway corporate, for example caring about shareholder value or returns on investment. Then ask yourself why you care about that, and so on, until you get to something more personal.

The benefits of asking questions.

When I was approaching 11 years old, I was due to be sitting those exams that determine which school you'd attend when you graduate in to secondary or high school. My two elder brothers had attended Sale Boys Grammar School and my father told me that if I too graduated to Sale Grammar, he'd give me £5. IN 1971, £5 bought a lot of candy! I passed my exam and won a bursary to another school, North Cestrian, where academic achievement was always expected to be higher. That summer, my father asked which of the schools I'd prefer to attend. I said Sale Grammar. £5 duly pocketed!

Move forward another eleven years, we were out walking as a family around Salisbury. My father sidled up to me and told me he had a question, one that he'd been wanting to ask for a long time. "Why did you choose Sale Grammar?" "Easy" I answered, "because you said you'd give me £5!"

"If you'd gone to North Cestrian I'd have given you £10, he answered"

I never ever forgot that lesson and have never shied away from asking questions since and it' is one reason I love coaching others, I can ask even the dumb questions that need to be asked, I can be provocative and challenging.

At the end of each section I'll be asking questions, obvious questions mostly, but ones which every time you intend to lead a project, task or challenge, or taker a new role or a new team, you can refer back here and go through each of the questions, one by one.

Context Questions

- What am I trying to achieve?

- What can I do to make this compelling

- Why am I trying to do this?

- What are the benefits of action/consequences of inaction?

- How can I show the maths?

- What objections might I face and how to acknowledge them?

- Why do I care?

Chapter 5: Credibility

"It takes a lot of effort to win back credibility after having lost it so heavily."

Giorgio Napolitano

It is clear from the research and good common-sense that employees want to be assured that their leaders know what they are doing, and in fact, are good at it. Of course, a well-known track record of successes is a useful thing to have rather than having to wave your curriculum vitae about; however for most of us, our track records are not always able to fully demonstrate capabilities. Especially when faced with a new job, new role, or new team, we have to be able to demonstrate our competence in a way that seeks to assure people that we are the right person to lead a team or a project, or indeed an entire business.

We have all met people that when they join a firm continue to declare, "When I was at ABC Corp, we always did things this way". Annoying! How can we share our credibility without sounding like the office bore, or without having to recite our CV every time we feel the need to demonstrate credibility?

The answers lie in story-telling and sharing of experiences. Rather than a list of whats, it's more to do with the hows and the learnings. Our track records tend to go before us; our new team have done their research and know what you've done, but not how. They know which school you went to but not that you captained the rugby team there to un-unbeaten home record. They know what you studied at University but not what your dissertation was on or the research that you did. Giving relevant examples that support your choices and serve to demonstrate prior learning, often through the power of story-telling will serve you well. Even if an example you give shows a weakness, yes that project failed, as long as you know why and can communicate that. Don't be shy about this; often we're too humble to blow our own trumpets. Even my own history, when learning to become a chef has relevance in what I do as a leadership and communication coach, the busy commercial kitchen has not one head chef, but a brigade of leaders and communicators, each playing an important role in delivering the best possible experience for its clientele, in a very high pressure environment.

Yet we often achieve our leadership positions because of our competence, engineers become chief engineers, accountants become CFO's and so on. We may have technical competence, but when it comes to leading people, we have to start developing a new set of competences that will need to be proven. We may move to a role because of previous leadership know-how, yet lack any technical knowledge. Sadly none of us are perfect, or maybe that's a good thing? Even our iconic CEO's like Jobs and Gates and our politicians like Obama and Thatcher are not perfect. Yet with imperfection come humility. A leader's ability to declare their shortcomings or gaps and ask for help really helps foster trust and humility. After all, you're human too right?

Go back to context, to reinforce your credibility when declaring the context; it helps if you have some experience of the history behind the problem or issue to be tackled. Perhaps you were the one who discovered or identified the issue. Describing that history and the effect it had on you, helps clarify your personal motivation and helps people to better understand the maths behind why you are making the recommendations that you are – or seeking advice and input.

There's also a place here for humility. Humility being the quality of not being proud because you are aware of your weaknesses or limitations. It is a dance between celebrating and sharing your successes whilst acknowledging your limitations. Leaders don't always have the answers or the skills or knowledge to carry out wat needs to be done. That's part of the reason they recruit others. In most organisations, when there is a change of Leadership, what often follows is a change in the leadership team, they recruit new people to the team who will complement their own skills and support them in the areas of weakness. Take it from Albert Einstein: "I have no special talent," he claimed, "I am only passionately curious."

I was recently asked to chair a strategy planning session for a global pharmaceutical business to help them sell their best-selling drug in the Czech Republic. I had to declare I had no idea about the drug or its application, not about the Czech Republic, and that what I'd bring to the event, was a curiosity and provocative approach to the planning process. I could ask the silly questions, challenge assumptions and work with a structure that would provide a result – with their help.

That dance between shouting about your successes, publicly learning from your failures and sharing your limitations, helps build your credibility as an authentic and honest leader.

Credibility Questions

- What skills do I bring to the issue?

- What history and experience do I have of the problem to be solved?

- What similar experiences have I encountered, what happened? Both positive and negative.

- What relevant qualifications do I hold and how do they apply in this case?

- What other experiences have I had that might add value?

- What are my limitations or weaknesses that I'm comfortable sharing?

- What help do I need?

Chapter 6: Character

Character is like a tree and reputation like a shadow. The shadow is what we think of it; the tree is the real thing.

Abraham Lincoln

People follow people. They do not often willingly follow job titles or corporations. Peoples' willingness to be influenced by you, to follow you begins with an individual's willingness to trust you. Their trust in you; the confidence that you are the right person to lead and that you will do the right things.

To trust that you are the right person in which to place their trust means that they need to know who you are. It's no longer a question of 'showing them who's Boss!' Today it's more of a question of 'showing them who the Boss really is. As we showed in the preface, trust indices show that we trust more, those people we know or think we know. So how do we show people that they 'know' us and that we deserve their trust?

First thing is first; you need to know yourself. Without that it will be nearly impossible for others to. People would like to know more about you, including your strengths, as well as your weaknesses; after all, none of us are perfect. This is an important point for leaders to be able to relate to others on a human level. People always like to know about your emotional side; what drives you, what disappoints you. People naturally like to know whether you're being consistent with who you really are, for as discussed previously consistency is a major component in the establishment of trust.

Integral to leadership are the relationships developed and they can only be great when there is two-way sharing. You need a little courage to take off the boss's mask, to let your guard down, showing your vulnerabilities. Additionally, you need a great sense of curiosity and questions developed to get those you seek to influence to also let down their guard. After all, what's at stake? If you don't share your weaknesses or vulnerabilities, people will either find them out and present them in a way not of your choosing, or even worse, make them up!

For the last twenty years Human Resource departments have made the recruitment and selection of new employees a science. Comparing data received with competency frameworks, analysing our preferences with psychometric tests and 'type indicators'. Yet, it's our own particular strengths AND weaknesses that make us unique. Psychometrics and models tend to put people in boxes, yet because of our uniqueness, we'd need today 7.4 Billion boxes for the categories to be accurate. What is unique about you, who are you, what are your own particular values and why? The way we 'show up to work' and the way we communicate our enthusiasm can really become quite contagious.

So often the unique character of the leader is what makes them attractive as a follower and because followers are unique too, they tend to be attracted to different types of leaders. Herb Kelleher from Southwest Airlines, very different from Donald Trump. Richard Branson, very different from Alan Sugar. I know who I'd prefer to work for, but hey, that's just me.

So, declare who you are, let people get close enough so that they experience you. Okay so you have 10,000 employees. Ryan Schneider, President of the card business at Capital One bank runs his own blog so that employees can read for themselves about his dogs, his favourite music and more.

Who am I? It's a tough question to answer. We are all symptoms of our upbringing. Our values are defined over a long period time with outside influences such as parents, siblings, the church, education, media and so on. To determine who you are so that you can share that is a process of self-analysis of determining what is important to us. Think about what you enjoy – what would you be doing if money were not an issue. Pay attention to those times when you lose yourself, because you're probably enjoying what you're doing – and if you can do more of it.

Once you have determined who you are, let your values guide you and learn to communicate through the lens of your values. What I mean by that is if you allow your values to guide your decision making process, let it be known that when making decisions, that what you have done.

And of course if you've not already answered the question "Why do you care?" – You can begin to do that – and it has been an eye opener for many when it comes to choosing or changing their career. I know one COO of a large private client wealth management business who just enjoyed meeting famous people after his father bought him an autograph book as a 7 year old.

There are many web sites and tools that can help you discover what's important to you and to prioritise those values. It will really help you answer the question of who you are. You can then use that knowledge to lead others from a personal stance rather than a positional stance.

The time comes now for you to step up to the plate, and lead. By signalling your own commitment to what it is you're trying to achieve, inspiring others by demonstrating how much skin you are prepared to put in to the game. If you truly believe in what you are setting out to achieve, then show it. The more personal your investment through time, personal money, effort, risk, the more likely others will follow to achieve your goals. At that point, once you've signalled your own commitment, then you can begin the process of asking others for their commitment.

Then, and only then, you can make the ultimate sacrifice of bestowing upon them, your followers, the recognition for successes – truly standing on the shoulders of those you seek to lead.

Once again, we have a place here for humility. Bestowing upon the others the recognition for effort and success says a lot about who you are and how you behave.

Everyone we seek to lead needs some 'stroking' from time to time – every day you should be seeking opportunities to tell people why their work is important and how it contributes. Giving relevant recognition for work well done.

And once again, there is a balance, give recognition too much and it de-values, giving recognition so some and not others fragments teams, giving public recognition when they don't like it or visa versa doesn't 'hit the right buttons' sometimes. Consistency and pertinence are critical.

Two examples – If you know me well enough there are two things I don't like. Heights and Fish! To celebrate a successful project completion one year I was taken for a trip on the London Eye and ten on to a seafood restaurant! Thanks!

The best piece of recognition – was from Stewart Miller, remember him? Asked one year to present at the annual conference on the Return on Investment in training, I was nervous but got through my presentation, and he walked behind me and just placed on hand on my shoulder. Not public, not spoken but his action meant everything and that was over 20 years ago and I'll never forget ow it made me feel.

Character Questions

- Who am I?

- What do I enjoy doing?

- What do I dislike doing?

- What are my values?

- Who has had the greatest impact on me and why?

- How do I measure personal success?

- How do I make decisions – both at home and work?

- Why do I care about what you're doing in the workplace?

- What skin am I willing to put in the game?

- How will I recognise the contributions of my followers?

Chapter 7: Communication

The single biggest problem in communication is the illusion that it has taken place.

George Bernard Shaw

The last and by no means least principle of trust and leadership is the ability to communicate, really, really well. In fact, in reality, it's the only principle, we use it to share our credentials, our character and use it to set the scene in context. In addition to what Shaw says above, it seldom works effectively as what we intend to communicate is exactly what's received.

The purpose of communication is to share as well as exchange ideas, emotions and feelings, concepts, information, stories, thoughts, values and opinions. Whilst this is not meant to be an exhaustive list, you get the idea. In short, we feel or think something and through speech, writing, non-verbal communication or images we share that. The receiver receives and then converts that to a thought of feeling that can be the same thought or feeling that we have or not. The problem is filters, the perceptions and assumptions that we all have, defined by our upbringing and teaching differ, thereby filtering differently and so the completeness of the message gets lost. It's like we're looking at things through different lenses. Then there's our ability to listen, properly.

We don't always set out to send a list of words or numbers to be retained or memorised and so too much use of words and/or data confuses.. We usually intend to communicate a feeling or emotion, a picture from the mind's eye or a sensation that triggers different reactions in the receiver.

Deciding what you want the receiver to experience is the first step in deciding which communication tool to use.

The first I'll walk about is Imagery and I'm talking about adding a piece of clipart to a PowerPoint presentation but rather the spoken imagery. The function of spoken imagery is to generate a vivid and graphic representation of what you can see and that appeals to as many of the receivers' senses as possible. So when telling a story about a previous project, or a customers' experience of service, you can appeal to the receivers sense of hearing, smell, taste as well as sight. This takes practice and also requires you to use not only words but hands and face too. To see this in practice, go to YouTube and watch Barack Obama's "Fire it up speech" – when he talks about a woman in Greenwood, I quote "And she's dressed like she just came from church — she's got a big church hat". People like Obama do this so well, they're practiced at it and it's very powerful.

A quick note about PowerPoint presentations, love them or hate them, no matter. The use of images on slides can also be powerful – every picture tells a story and can often tap in to a part of the brain in the receiver that bullet points alone cannot do. But beware of over use.

Similarly, the use of metaphors and analogies also connect with the brain where you can feel the sense of urgency or desperation that is driving the need for change in a way that data cannot.

Body language and emotions play a big part in Leadership; it's the way we can allow others to see our energy, our enthusiasm, our frustration and any other emotions we wish to share. It has often been cited that emotional intelligence is a far more accurate predictor of leadership capability that anything else. So when communicating, learn to use your own emotions in a planned and structured way. This means learning to listen to your own emotions and then rationalise a considered response to situations rather than reacting, which our emotions would prefer to do! It also means we can focus our energies on using constructive emotions to convey our messages.

Personally speaking, Listening is the one skill, that as a human race, we are dreadful at! I used to coach rugby to 8 year olds and I thought they were bad! Rather than writing about active listening, here are the top tips when listening.

1. Be doing something else - typically, when on the phone, keep reading emails or typing, people will know — try standing up when on the phone, it removes distractions.
2. Listen with your eyes as well as you ears.

3. Don't interrupt – it just says "I'm more important than you."

4. Assume intent – this can lead to all kinds of problems. Always assume noble intent, at least at the start.

5. Summarising or questioning can be useful to confirm that you've heard and understand – also gives you time to plan your responses.

And remember – communication is a two-way process and listening is not the same as hearing.

Communication Questions

- Who am I communicating with and what will they want?

- What tools can I use to best communicate my messages?

- Why do I care and what emotions do I have that I can share?

Chapter 8: Summary

Trust is not a right that you earn because you have a corner office or a key to the executive bathroom. Leadership is not leadership unless you have committed followers. Both need to be earned and can easily be lost. These tools of creating a context that others can see and feel, building your personal credibility, sharing a little more about who you are, and communicating really well, all take practice. And practice comes from applying those tools regularly and of course, when appropriate.

The key to using these tools is not to use them in a linear fashion, not to use them all at once. The key is to choose the right tool for the job, just as mechanic or brain surgeon chooses their tools carefully when presented with differing challenges.

That said, you need to have answers to as many questions as I've asked, prepared as much as possible. Preparation, every time you seek to influence or lead others or earn some credits in your trust bank account will be critical.

Whenever you see leaders who you admire just 'pull it off' so effortlessly, it's no doubt the result of preparation and practice. Even then, just sometimes it doesn't work. We all lose faith in our leaders from time to time, it's are to find a politician we wish we still had. Things go wrong, the odds can be stacked against them, external influences can be disastrous. In those situations, it's how you handle them that really counts. We're human are are entirely fallible, and yet, that's quite nice.

Anyone can be a leader and you don't need the job title to be one either. It takes a little courage at times to take the first step or speak up when something needs saying. It takes self-awareness, humility and practice.

I wish you well in your ventures and thank you for reading this and if you are ever in doubt – ask!

Your humble servant
Andrew Wallbridge

Andrew is a leadership and senior team development coach and facilitator.

Drawing a firm distinction between developing leadership skills, and developing Leaders, Andrew has worked with some of the world's leading global organisations in the areas of leadership, service quality and employee engagement, and worked alongside

many prominent Leadership Commentators. His passion lies in helping business leaders create and communicate visions, develop leadership skills and aligning processes and procedures to organisational intent.

Andrew contracts his work to several consulting firms and runs his own clients through http://WorkSmart.global from his home in South Wales.

www.ingramcontent.com/pod-product-compliance
Lightning Source LLC
Chambersburg PA
CBHW071839200526
45169CB00020B/1950